# SANCTIF

# AND

# PERFECTION

## E.W. BULLINGER

ISBN: 978-1-78364-503-9

## www.obt.org.uk

**The Open Bible Trust**
**Fordland Mount, Upper Basildon,**
**Reading, RG8 8LU, UK.**

# SANCTIFICATION AND PERFECTION

## CONTENTS

\*\*\*\*\*\*\*\*\*\*

# SANCTIFICATION.

# SANCTFICATION.

This is one of the four things which God has made Christ to be unto His people. They are "Wisdom, and Righteousness, and Sanctification, and Redemption" (1 Cor. 1:30).

It is a common practice with those who do not see the truth of "the two natures"[1] to constantly speak of Sanctification as if it were a progressive work by which the Old nature is constantly improved until it is made meet for the inheritance of the saints (*i.e., sanctified ones*) in light.

But the opposite is the fact, Scripture never speaks of "a change of heart." That is man's formula. God speaks of a "new heart" being created: but never of the old heart "changed." True, with Israel in the coming day of blessing, the heart will be exchanged – the stony heart for a heart of flesh, but even that will not be the "change" of one into the other. The Holy Spirit never speaks of His work as being the improvement of the Old nature, on the contrary, He tells us that the old man is hostile to God (Rom. 8:7): that he cannot get to know spiritual things; that they are foolishness to him (1 Cor. 2:14).

From this it is surely clear that if the natural man can neither "receive" nor "get to know the things of the Spirit

---

[1] For more on this see *The Two Natures in the Child of God* by E W Bullinger, details of which can be seen at the end of this book.

of God," how can he be sanctified? The flesh is eternally opposed to the spirit; *i.e.*, the Old nature is eternally opposed to spirit, which is the New nature, as Gal. 5:17 testifies. Conflict is not Sanctification! Neither is the Spirit of God in His operations in our New nature improving that with which He is carrying on a warfare.

Those who are looking for Sanctification as a progressive work are looking for a ground of peace in a sanctified nature, instead of being occupied with that peace which has been made by the perfect sacrifice of Christ. Instead of being occupied with Christ's finished work *for* them, they are taken up with an ever-unfinished work in them. It is a question of Christ or self; and the only reason why multitudes of Christians are occupied with progressive sanctification is because it exalts self. Whereas the work of the Spirit is just the opposite – viz.: to glorify Christ. "He shall glorify me" were the Saviour's words (John 16:14), and in them we have a standard by which we may test everything in us and around us.

"But OF HIM are ye in Christ Jesus, who of God is made unto us . . . Sanctification." This is one of four things which we have in Christ. Christ is made unto us "Righteousness." How? and When? By our works? By anything we can do? Righteousness is expressly declared to be "to him that worketh not" (Rom. 4:5). So it is with all that we have "in Christ." As it is with Righteousness, so it must be with Sanctification. Righteousness is declared to be "without works," but most Christians today want to have Sanctification *by works*. But Sanctification is put on precisely the same ground as Righteousness. As we get the one, so do we get the other, for we get both in

Christ. Surely our readers must see that we can no more work out a Sanctification for ourselves than we can work out a Righteousness of our own.

True, it is written of holiness – "without which no man can see the Lord" (Heb. 12:14). It does not say, without a certain measure of holiness, but without the thing itself. How then are we to get it? the answer is: - In precisely the same way that we get Righteousness, - *in Christ*! We get Christ by gift, by grace, and by imputation, and it is all Christ from first to last. *Our standing* is in all His perfection. There is only one standing for every saved sinner. We cannot grow in this standing. It is perfect. Nothing can be put to it and nothing can be taken from it; our knowledge of it and experience of it, and our enjoyment of it may grow and will grow. But it is one standing and the same standing for the weakest, poorest, youngest, humblest child of God as well as for the highest and most learned. It is not a question of knowledge, but of life. And that life is Christ. In Him we have got a perfect righteousness by grace. In Him also we have a perfect Sanctification by grace – Righteous before God, as He is righteous: Holy before God, as He is holy, because Christ *"is made"* both to us. Both are perfect. So that the child of God is wholly righteous and wholly sanctified, and his standing is perfect, eternal and unchangeable because it is Divine.

True, our *walk* is marked by failures, and infirmities, and falls and sins. This is a quite different matter; our walk is quite distinct from our standing in Christ and cannot affect it in the slightest degree.

"MADE MEET." This is the absolute truth as to the present position of all who are in Christ as the result of His eternally perfect work for us. And it is occupation with Him and with what God has made us to be in Him that will cause us and enable us to "walk worthy of His calling".

It will not be brought about by occupation with our walk.

We do not live by the study of biology, or breathe by the study of pneumatics, or hear by the study of acoustics, or get warm by studying the theory of heat. In like manner we cannot grow by trying to add one cubit to our height: or add one year to our life by "taking thought" about it.

How then can our *walk* be made worthy of our calling? Only by the word of Christ dwelling in us richly: only by the application of that word to our hearts. Hence it is written: "Sanctify them through Thy truth: Thy word is truth" (John 17:17). It is the special office of the Holy Spirit to constantly apply this Word to us. Hence, "God hath from the beginning chosen you to salvation through sanctification of the Spirit and belief of the truth" (2 Thess. 2:13).

But this is not any attempt to improve our walk. Thus occupied, the New nature feeds and grows and becomes strong. There will be growth here, but, as to our standing in Christ, that is perfect and in Him we are righteous and holy in all His righteousness and all His holiness.

# "MADE MEET."

# "MADE MEET."

Religion, as distinct from Christianity, is known by several unmistakable marks.

1. It gives its votaries plenty to *believe*. It makes large demands upon their credulity. Whether in India, China, Rome or England there is a great deal that has to be swallowed.

2. It gives its votaries plenty to *do*. Works of all and many kinds are demanded; and gifts and payments have to be made. These works are incessant and unceasing.

3. But Religion gives its votaries very little *to hope for*. From the Chinese heavens, which are entered according to merit, to the Mohammedan heaven of glorified licentiousness; Rome's Purgatory and "four last things," and the heaven of unconverted Protestants, which consists chiefly in meeting one's relations again by some "fountain" or at some "gate" In all these there is very little hope for compared with "that blessed hope" revealed in the Gospel.

4. But one of the greatest contrasts consists in this – *uncertainty as to salvation*! In this, Religion and Christianity are exactly opposite. You may always know the profession of religion by this mark. They all practically deny that Christ's work IS finished,

that redemption has been accomplished and that salvation was completed at the Cross, that He came "to save His people," and He saved them. That is why religious people today, talk about people being "saved" *now*, not knowing that all who are "in Christ" were saved on Calvary.

Even the most religious among Protestant Evangelicals, if asked whether they really believe when they profess and confess again and again with their lips – "I believe in the forgiveness of sins" – will seldom get beyond "I hope so," or the assertion that "No one can ever know" in this life. They can never speak with certainty about it. Some call this humility and are proud of it, thinking it presumption to take the ground which the grace of God in Christ Jesus has given to us.

But this brings us to the contrast between all this and the Christianity which is revealed in the Church Epistles.

1. Christianity gives us the simplest possible matter to believe. We have to "believe God," *i.e.*, what God says and has said in His Word and it is counted to us for righteousness (Rom. 4:20-24).

2. It gives us nothing whatever to do for salvation, for Christ has "done it all, long ago"; and what is now done by those who are saved is the irrepressible outcome of the New nature, which knows no joy equal to this.

3. It gives us a great and blessed hope, consisting of "exceeding great and precious promises." The hope of being caught up to meet the Lord in the air and so of ever being with the Lord, glorified with His own glory.

4. But beside all this, it gives us now and here a blessed certainty as to our present accomplished salvation and a sweet enjoyment of it in our souls.

All who are in Christ are the happy possessors of the New nature, by which they are able to see the incorrigible character of the Old nature (Rom. 8:7), and in which they have a standard by which to test it; and have a daily evidence that in ourselves "dwelleth no good thing" (Rom. 7:8). Consequently, while religious people never rise higher than an effort to improve the Old nature, the true Christian has learned that the Old nature cannot please God (Rom. 8:8), that it is hostile to God, and is not subject to the law of God, neither indeed can be (Rom. 8:7). While this fills him with daily conflict and at times with much distress, yet it is his one great ground of assurance, the blessed evidence that he is the happy possessor of this wondrous "gift of God" (Rom. 6:23; Eph. 2:8), otherwise he would not know either his ruined condition as to himself, or the perfect standing which he has in Christ.

This was the position of the saints in Colosse and ought to be the position of every true Christian today. The Epistle addressed to them begins with "Grace": grace which meets with us as lost, delivers us, cleanses us and sets us in perfect freedom before God our Father. God reveals it, Faith enjoys it and sets aside all reasoning from feelings or experience.

The saints in Colosse [Colossians 1] are addressed as being "in Christ" (v. 2) and therefore as "complete in Him" (v. 9). "In whom WE HAVE redemption through his blood, even the forgiveness of sins" (v. 14). "Who HATH delivered us from the power of darkness and HATH translated us into the kingdom of His beloved Son" (v. 13).

Thus we are assured of, and are dealt with as having, *present redemption, present deliverance, and present translation.*

And more than this. Those who possess such wondrous unmeasured blessedness, can only worship. We have nothing to ask or pray for as to our *standing in Christ*. This, we are assured, is "complete, in Him" (v. 9), nothing can add to this completeness. We cannot ever grow or increase in it. We can increase in our enjoyment and appreciation of it, but we cannot grow in our relationship to God or our standing in Christ.

Of course, as to our walk and our whole path, now upon earth, it is true that in everything by prayer and supplication we are to let our requests be made known unto God; but if we realise our standing, our prayers will be full of praise, because our heart is so full of rest, and our cup so overflowing with blessing.

Hence, in verse 12, the prayer of the Apostle by the Holy Ghost for us is that we may be occupied in "giving thanks unto the Father, which HATH MADE US MEET to be partakers of the inheritance of the saints in light." Surely we are overwhelmed by "the riches of the grace" which hath done such great things for us.

How few, even of the Lord's own saved ones, know anything of the extent of the "riches" which are theirs! How few are engaged in counting over and dwelling upon this wealth of grace! Selfishness occupies their thoughts with *themselves* and *their* walk; and hence, the inevitable result is that they are looking for some work *yet to be done* in them or by them to make them meet. Some think that affliction and trials help to do this; others think that holiness of life will do something for them, not seeing that they *have been* now already "made meet" for glory, and not realising that it is something not *to be* done, but which *has been* done.

The solemn fact is that all such, not only lose the peace blessing and enjoyment of present certainty as to their standing; but, by taking up a position which implies the possibility of anything being able to add one iota to our meetness for Heaven, they (1) deny the truth as to the ruin of man in the flesh. (2) they set aside the work of God in having made us new creations in Christ. and (3) they call in question the full value of the work of Christ who "by one offering HATH perfected forever them that are sanctified." (Heb. 10:14).

There is no limitation in these words in Col. 1. They are true of the veriest babe in Christ; of the humblest, poorest, weakest, and most ignorant believer, because they speak of and refer to *the work of God in Christ*, and not to our own abilities or attainments. True we may forget this, we may have doubts and fears, and we may through our infirmities be conscious of many failures, but these do not and cannot for one moment affect the work of God in Christ.

No! ours is now a *present meetness*, always a perfect meetness. Oh! what rest for the heart! What peace for the mind, and all the work and gift of the Father, and all "in Christ" (Eph. 1:2).

We wait for the redemption of our body: we wait for the inheritance itself. But as to the forgiveness of ALL our sins, righteousness, sanctification, union with Christ, identification with Christ, completeness in Him, perfection in Him, *we do not wait for this*, because we have it all now, for it is written "who HATH MADE US MEET to be partakers of the inheritance of the saints in light." (Col. 1:12.)

# "IN HIS STEPS."

# "IN HIS STEPS."

The use which has been made of these words shows the importance of never interpreting or putting any meaning on a sentence until we see its place in the immediate context. If this be not done we are in imminent danger of ignorantly wresting the Word of God; and of perverting its true interpretation by introducing a meaning of our own quite foreign to the subject which is being treated of and quite beside the point which is being made.

1 Pet. 2:19-23, affords a valuable illustration. The subject of the context is "suffering" and "glory." It is an exhortation to bear suffering for well-doing patiently, remembering the "glory" which is to follow:

> "For this is thankworthy, if a man for conscience toward God endure grief, suffering wrongfully. For what glory is it, if, when ye be buffeted for your faults, ye shall take it patiently? But if, when ye do well and suffer for it, ye take it patiently, this is acceptable with God. For even hereunto were ye called." (1 Pet. 2:19-21a.)

And then an illustration and example is introduced to enforce this weighty exhortation: -

> "Because Christ also suffered for us, leaving us an example, that ye should follow his steps!" (1 Pet. 2:21.)

And then steps are defined and described, showing that they were the same steps as were referred to in the exhortation.

> "Who did no sin, neither was guile found in his mouth; who when he was reviled, reviled not again; when he suffered, he threatened not; but committed himself to him that judgeth righteously." (1 Pet. 2:22-23.)

Thus, the context makes the sense perfectly clear. Observe, it is "CHRIST" who was once here, but is here no longer, having been exalted and glorified, whose steps we are to follow; and not "Jesus" merely, who was once here in the days of his humiliation and sufferings. It is the "glory" which He has received on account of His suffering for well doing, which is to be before our minds; rather than his suffering steps when here upon earth.

If, when we are reviled we revile not again; if, when we suffer, we threaten not, but commit ourselves to him that judgeth righteously, we shall then follow His steps.

There is no such collocation of words as "in His steps." It is a non-scriptural expression. We are to follow after or upon His steps; those steps which are defined, steps of suffering for well-doing, being assured of a like glory which shall assuredly follow the sufferings.

Those who are thus exhorted are those who are described as "elect according to the fore-knowledge of God the Father, through sanctification of the spirit unto obedience and sprinkling of the blood of Jesus Christ" (1 Pet. 1:2).

These and these alone are able to receive this exhortation, and only to these is it addressed. It is a perversion of this exhortation to apply it indiscriminately to the unconverted! And it is this very perversion which makes it popular. It brings plenty of that which looks like "well-doing," but there is no "suffering" with it. It lacks the Divine "Hallmark" of true "well-doing" which is "the reproach of Christ" (Heb. 11:26). The 4,000,000 readers of the popular religious novel to which we refer will get none of "His reproach" (Heb. 13:13). No, they will get "the praise of men," not the hatred of the world; not any of that "suffering" which can be endured only under the assurance of coming "glory."

They will bring that Blessed and Holy one down to their own level and ask what He would do! They will exalt "man" in whose interest all this "well-doing" is to be undertaken but they will at the same time deceive their own souls and pervert the Word of God.

For, how can poor ignorant man know what He would do? How can a servant know what his master or her mistress would do? In the absence of the mistress, would the servant preside at the family table? For *that* is what the mistress would do. In the absence of the master, would the servant give orders or sign cheques? He had better not do it; he had better not do anything beyond what he is *specially instructed to do*.

He had better not follow his own fancy or imagination as to what his master would do.

How marvelous is the pride of the poor human heart. He calls that Blessed one "Jesus," and like another Judas, he says "Hail MASTER!" while, by the very act, he drags him below the level of all earthly masters, treats him as a servant, and asks what the Master would do, Whom he has just put back again in the place of a servant!

There is something subtle and Satanic in this attitude of heart. The real reason for it is not ostensibly to bring Jesus down to be a servant again, but, hailing Him as "Master," the real object is to exalt self into that position.

It is so. For, "what would Jesus do?" Well, He would not marry. He would not have where to lay His head. He would be more homeless than foxes and birds. They have their holes and their nests, but "He had nowhere to lay His head."

Are these some of the "steps" that the Sheldonites propose to "walk in"? Are they going to preach universal celibacy and give up their comfortable homes? No! they will pick and choose the "steps," and they will choose any except those specially mentioned in the context of 1 Pet. 2:21, because these are connected with "the offence of the cross," and "the reproach of Christ." These will bring the hatred of the world. The world knew him not. And the same world today does not know those who *really* "follow His steps." But it *does* know, and will love and honour, those who walk in their own steps while they call them "His."

# THE GUILTY
# BY NO MEANS
# CLEARED.

# THE GUILTY BY NO MEANS CLEARED.

This is the assertion of Jehovah in Ex. 34:7, in proclaiming His name and His attributes.

Moses had asked, in Ex. 33:18: "Show me thy glory." Jehovah had replied in the next verse, "I will make all my goodness pass before thee." And the promise is fulfilled in 34:5-7, when He descended in the cloud . . . and proclaimed the name of Jehovah.

So that in these words, "and will by no means clear the guilty." we have part of the very glory and goodness of God.

It is as much God's *goodness* as it is His *glory* to not clear the guilty."

Jehovah tells us not only *what* He will not do, but *why* He will not do it.

This does not mean that there is any unwillingness on His part to show mercy. On the contrary, it is declared (Ps. 86:5) "Thou, Lord, art good and ready to forgive." Nothing that we can do can make Him more ready than He is to do all His will.

It is, however, here, not a mere question of *forgiveness*, but of atonement. The word is Hebrew (*nakee*) and its meaning may be traced from Gen. 24:8: "Then their name shall be *clear* from this mine oath": Gen. 44:10 "Ye shall be *blameless*"; Ex. 20:7: "*guiltless*"; Ex. 21:28: "The owner of the ox shall be *quit*": Ex. 23:7: "*innocent.*"

It means, therefore, that God will not forgive without satisfaction made to justice. He will be "faithful and just" in the forgiveness of sins (1 John 1:9).

There can be no display of mercy at the expense of justice.

A penalty has been fixed upon sin, and Jehovah will never pronounce the sentence of acquittal except in full accordance with justice in the payment of that penalty.

And yet the world's religion is based on the very opposite of this fundamental truth of the Gospel.

The world believes that God will clear the guilty, i.e. everyone, as God is love and God is merciful! This is the source of the delusion, as is the view that the sinner can, by his own meritorious conduct and repentance and "works," obtain mercy. This is the cause of all the deceptive resting in ordinances that we see around us.

It is only a half-gospel, leading to a false peace, to declare to sinners and the world at large that "God is love." To begin God's gospel here is to begin building from the top. It is not so begun in Romans 1, when God lays the true foundation. He does not separate the two great truths. He does not reveal His "righteousness" apart from His "*wrath.*" See Rom. 1:16, 17.

It is our place, therefore, to proclaim that *God is just*, "and that He will by no means clear the guilty"; because on this foundation we can at once proceed to build. It is the very foundation of the truth that "God is love." For if there were the clearing of the guilty, if there were acquittal, apart from law, if there were any such conniving at sin, it would be treating it as a light thing and putting a premium on sin, and we should lose the very ground of the manifestation of God's holy love, which is not manifested to us apart from Christ.

Apart from Christ, "the Lord is a man of war," revealing His wrath against all ungodliness and unrighteousness. But it is in Christ that He is seen as the God of peace, revealing His love by imputing the sins of His people to Christ.

What a wondrous truth! Sin imputed to Him who "knew no sin," who "did no sin," who was "holy, harmless and undefiled."

Yes, the sins of His people were indeed laid to His charge, and he was dealt with as guilty.

And when even He was dealt with as guilty, He was by no means cleared! He drank the bitter cup to the dregs! He paid the uttermost farthing! He endured the penalty for all the guilt of all His people. Not some of the penalty for all men, but all the penalty for some, yea many, even all His people.

That holy and blessed One was not cleared! And if any now are determined to bear their own guilt, it is perfectly certain that they will never be cleared.

What blessedness, then, there is in these words in Ex. 34:7, when we read them in connection with the revelation of God's gospel as declared in the Epistle to the Romans.

How full of encouragement for us. Do we sometimes say – when we see ourselves in the light which He shines upon us and in us – 'How can he clear me? I am all guilt. When I think of all His goodness, which has been leading me and following me, how can he clear me?'

Ah! The answer of God's gospel comes to us and answers all our questions, removes all our doubts, calms all our fears. Jehovah transferred all my sins to Christ! And when they were laid upon Him *He was not cleared*! Therefore, the penalty has been borne, the heavy debt has been paid. He bore the wrath, He endured the curse and the blessed consequences is that I (and all such) stand before God *without a spot*, righteous in Christ's righteousness; accepted in all His acceptableness; perfect in Christ Jesus, complete in Him; yea, holy in His holiness, and only waiting to be glorified with His glory.

It is almost beyond belief. When we realise it only in part it seems almost too good to be true.

What! Will He never condemn me? "No condemnation"? Not, though I see that in myself every day and every hour I am deserving of all condemnation? What! Does He stoop to my infirmities and bear with my frailties? Yes! It is true! He will by no means break His word. He laid all my sins upon my Substitute, and when He bore them, *He was not cleared.*

Oh, what a blessed truth. Every sin, every iniquity, every transgression, every backsliding, every thought, word and deed, all foreknown and laid on Him, who, though He knew the awful burden He had to bear, did not withdraw His neck from the yoke, but drank the cop of wrath to the dregs that He might give now to His church and people the cup of blessing for all eternity.

In Him we were not cleared: for in Him we died and in Him we are risen again. Neither the Law nor death has any further claim upon us or power over us. Though "it is appointed unto all men once to die," there is really, now no reason why we should ever die at all. All who are "in Christ" have already died in Him, and in Him they are risen again, and only wait for Ascension, and not death. If they are called to fall asleep, it will be only sleep; they will soon wake again when He comes forth into the air and sounds forth His great assembling shout, and then they will be caught up to meet Him in the air, and so to be ever with the Lord.

How blessed the thought, yea, the fact, that we are not merely pardoned for having got into debt, but that the debt has been paid and our liability cleared and that a Risen Christ is our receipt for payment in full! Not merely pardoned, but justified; not merely justified, but accepted; and accepted too in Christ as He is accepted with the

Father, and have Him not merely *substituted* for us, but ourselves identified with Him.

What a precious truth for us to dwell upon in the trials of life, in our seasons of depression in a sick room or on a dying bed. To know that I am cleared because the Lord Jesus was not; that I am acquitted because He was dealt with as guilty. May the Lord carry home His own word and truth with Power to our hearts and He shall have all the praise.

# "BE PERFECT."

# "BE PERFECT."

The command of the Lord Jesus in John 5:39, that we should "Search the Scriptures" can be obeyed with great profit and blessing in connection with these words. There are strong grammatical reasons for taking this word "search" as *imperative.* for the indicative mood rarely, if ever, stands at the beginning of a sentence without the pronoun or some other word to indicate it. Further, the word "search" here means *to trace* or *track out* as a dog or a lion traces out its prey by following the scent. So here it tells us that we are to *trace out* this word "be perfect" and follow it up and track it out and thus learn its lessons from the use which the Holy Spirit has made of it.

The word rendered *be perfect* here (2 Cor. 13:11), is (*katartizo)*; and its lessons may be learned by nothing some of the passages where it occurs. We will put the various English renderings in **bold** type.

1. Matt. 4:21: "And going on from thence, he saw other two brethren, James the son of Zebedee, and John his brother, in a ship with Zebedee their father, **mending** their nets."

Here the word is rendered *mending*; and hence, we are taught that, *to be perfect*, we are *to get mended* as to our walk, our works and our ways. The verb in 2 Cor. 13:11 is in the passive voice and means *to get mended,* not merely *to mend*, as though the action were our own – for we are like the nets, in Matt. 4:21, and we need another hand, yea, a Divine hand, to be put forth upon us. He alone can see the rents and the defects, He alone can see the danger arising to ourselves, from our habits of thought, our modes of speech, our methods of work; and He alone can repair what is broken and supply what is lacking so that we may be fitted for the use to which He would put us, and for the service in which He would employ us. Thus *mended* we shall "be perfect" in the sense in which the precept is given in 2 Cor. 13:11.

2. Rom. 9:22. Here we read of "the vessels of wrath **fitted** to (or for) destruction."

Destruction is all that these vessels are *fitted* for, and all that they are *fit* for. Hence, in the opposite direction, to be *fitted* for the work for which God has, in infinite grace, chosen us, is to be perfect according to 2 Cor. 13:11. This is the prayer on our behalf, that by the graces and gifts of the Holy Spirit we may bear faithful testimony and render faithful service for Christ the Lord. The end of all testimony is the glory of God in Christ, and if we are *fitted* for this by "the Spirit of truth" then we are perfect in the sense of 2 Cor. 13:11.

Do we ask how may we be thus *fitted?* The answer is, only by fellowship with Christ the Living Word: only by diligent study of the Scriptures – the written Word: only by making them the one object of our lives, and having the word of Christ dwelling richly within us. Thus and thus alone shall we be *fitted* for His service.

3. 1 Cor. 1:10: "Now I beseech you, brethren, by the name of our Lord Jesus Christ, that . . . there be no

divisions among you; but that ye **be-perfectly-joined-together** in the same judgment."

Here, the meaning receives further light. *To be perfect* means not to be divided, but united. This we shall be if our one object be Christ and our desire that of Paul when he said, "that I may know Him" (Phil. 3:10). It does not refer necessarily to outward unity. This seems to be man's only idea of union. The children of God are "all one in Christ," and there is no other union or bond of union. Man makes up his "divisions," and all within these he considers to be "united" or "in fellowship." But none of these barriers can separate, none of these folds can contain and include the whole "flock of God." Scattered and dispersed among all man's "divisions" will be found the members of the one Body and these are *"perfectly-joined-together* in Christ their head. They are all of "the same mind" as to His glorious person; they are all of "the same judgment" as to His perfect work. They have one *standing,* "found in HIM" (Phil. 3:9); one *object,* "that I may know HIM" (Phil. 3:10); and one blessed hope, to "look for the Saviour, the Lord Jesus Christ" . . . and to be made like HIM, for He shall at His coming "change our vile body, that it may be made like unto His glorious body" (Phil. 3:20, 21).

4. Gal. 6:1: "Brethren, if a man be overtaken in a fault, ye who are spiritual, **restore** such an one in the spirit of meekness: considering thyself, lest thou also be tempted."

This tells us that though we are perfect as to our *standing* in Christ it is far otherwise with us as to our walk on earth.

Hence, this gracious provision for our deepest need: - "He restoreth my soul" (Ps. 23:3). This is the special work of the great Shepherd Himself, and those who are "spiritual" are graciously permitted, yea are exhorted, to walk in His steps in this matter. He restores us – considering ourselves. The spiritual are to restore us, considering *themselves*! How vast the difference.

Alas! Alas! Where are the "spiritual"? Where are we to look for them? Where do we see their spiritual efforts in obeying this precious word? Alas! we say again, they seem to read this verse as though it were written "If a man be overtaken in a fault, ye who are righteous judge such an one; spread abroad the sad news; each one tell the other 'not to say anything,' and above all 'do not say that I told you'; follow up 'such an one,' injure him (not in the spirit of meekness) all you can; don't restore him, but cast him out: *not considering yourselves.*"

This is how Christians, today, try to "be perfect," and it is about the only thing in which they do actually reach "perfection" in the flesh. Yes, it is indeed "in the flesh" and of the flesh. For it is not the work of "ye who are spiritual."

*Restoration*, then is one of the shades of meaning which this word has, and a comparison of this with the other passages will help to complete the picture. God grant that some "spiritual" may be found among us; and if any of us shall be tried, and be betrayed into some error in doctrine, or some evil in practice, oh! that some gentle hand may be found to so minister the precious word of God in the spirit of meekness, that we may be restored.

But when we reflect on and contrast the perfectness of the Great Shepherd we would fain exclaim with David "Let us fall now into the hand of the Lord: for very great are His mercies: and *let me not fall into the hand of man*" (1 Chron. 21:13). For Jehovah my Shepherd is JEHOVAH-ROPHECA, who saith "I am the Lord that healeth thee," and of Him we can ever say, "He restoreth my soul."

5. Heb. 10:5. "A body hast thou **prepared** me" (lit., didst thou prepare me).

The human body of the Lord Jesus was, while perfectly human, specially *prepared* by the Holy Ghost; as is plainly stated in Luke 1:35: "The Holy Ghost shall come upon thee, and the power of the Highest shall overshadow thee: wherefore also that holy thing which shall be born of thee shall be called the Son of God."

Acceptable sacrifice and service can be rendered to God only by the preparation power of the Holy Spirit. Only those works are "good works" which God hath *prepared* for us to walk in" (Eph. 2:10). There are "wicked works" (Col. 1:21); and there are "dead works" (Heb. 6:1; 9:14). But only those are "good" which are wrought by the New nature, and therefore are "prepared" by God Himself. "The flesh profiteth nothing." And therefore no eloquence, no genius, no learning, no wisdom, if it proceeds only from the Old nature, is of any avail. It must be "power from on high" (Acts 1:8, compare Luke 1:35). What a comfort for us to know that this "power" does not depend on our attainments, but upon God's grace and gift; and that the humblest and weakest believer may be used by God and made to surpass the greatest human achievements, because it is work for eternity and not for time.

"The preparations of the heart in man . . . is from the Lord" (Prov. 16:1), and he who is thus *prepared* by the Holy Spirit is *perfect* in the sense of 2 Cor. 13:11.

> 6. Heb. 11:3 we read "By faith we understand that the worlds were **framed** by the word of God" (*i.e.*), were *prepared* or constituted. We learn ","by faith," that the ages and dispensations were *before-ordained* and *prepared* and *perfectly-joined-together* by the word of God. We also learn that the things which are seen have their being, not out of things which do appear. As to the things which are seen, they came into being not through any theories of evolution, not through any conjectures of geology. And as to the things that are not seen, through faith in the Divine testimony we understand and apprehend that all the ages and dispensations and times and seasons were all *prepared* and ordained by God; and made by Him. Neither were prepared by the blind laws of Nature or the vagaries of chance, but by the will and mandate of Jehovah who "spake and it was done."

What we learn from this is that, if our faculties of soul and body are to be brought into order it must be by the same Divine Mandate. If our times and seasons and comings and goings are to be reduced to order it must be by the will and word of Jehovah.

If our ways and works are to be controlled, not by any natural laws in the spiritual world, but by spiritual laws in the natural world; not by the opinion of men, but by the word of God, then we are "perfect" in the sense of 2 Cor. 13:11.

- May we, ourselves and our readers be thus perfected: *i.e.* may our walk be constantly *repaired.*
- May we be *fitted* for all our duties by the Holy Spirit.
- May we be *perfectly-joined-together* in Christ and in His truth.
- May we be ever *restored* by the Great Shepherd who seeks and finds his wandering sheep.
- May we be *prepared* for all emergencies and endued to meet them with "power from on high."

This is our desire, and this is our prayer This too, is the teaching of the Holy Spirit as to our perfection. Never once does He use the word, either in the original or in the English, to imply any change of the flesh unto spirit, or of the old nature unto the new, or of any change of heart. Never does He contemplate us as being in any condition which does not need *repairing, re-storing, fitting, or preparing,* and we may bless His holy name that these are the very needs for which He has so amply provided.

# THE CHURCH
# AT CORINTH.

# THE CHURCH AT CORINTH.

Paul tells the Corinthian saints (chap. 3:9, 10), "ye are God's building," and "I have laid the "foundation." This being so, it is evident that the believers in the land of Israel, under the ministry of the twelve apostles could *neither be the Church* as the Body of Christ, *nor represent* it, in the sense in which the Church was spoken of by Paul in his epistles as the Temple of God; for the building could not exist until the foundation was laid, and the foundation was not laid until Peter's ministry as recorded was ended.

The truth concerning Jesus, the Son of God and the value of His one offering for believers individually, is given us in the Epistles to the Romans and to the Hebrews. Justification is the subject of the Epistle to the Romans. "Being justified freely by His grace through the redemption that is in Christ Jesus" (chap. 3:24), "justified by His blood" (chap. 5:9). Sanctification is the subject of the Epistle to the Hebrews. "Both He that sanctifieth and they who are sanctified are all of one" (chap. 2:11). "By which will (of God) we are sanctified through the offering of the body of Jesus Christ once" (chap. 10:10). "Jesus that He might sanctify the people with His own blood, suffered without the gate" (chap. 13:12). It is in these truths that the Church of God is built up among the Gentiles as the Temple of God upon the foundation that

"Jesus Christ is the Son of the living God," so that the Church is the Temple of the living God (2 Cor. 6:16).

So, Paul addresses the saints at Corinth as "the Church of God which is at Corinth, to them that are sanctified in Christ Jesus, called saints, with all that in every place call upon the name of Jesus Christ our Lord, both theirs and ours." They own Him as their Lord in whom they are sanctified. They are "called to fellowship with the Son of God" (chap. 1:9). Not in His relation to Jerusalem, but to His Father, and in the value of His offering who suffered without the gate to sanctify them, in obedience to the will of God.

That the believers are justified in Christ is a "truth according to the prophets," for Isaiah has said (chap. 45:25): "In the Lord shall all the seed of Israel be justified and shall glory." This truth had been preached by Paul at Antioch in Pisidia (Acts 13:39). But that the believers from among the Gentiles were to be sanctified in Christ is a truth "according to the revelation of the mystery which was kept secret since the world began." This is now "made manifest"; for the first declared characteristic of the Church of God is that they are "sanctified in Christ."

The offering of the body of Jesus that He might sanctify the people by His own blood was accomplished "without the gate" of the city. "Therefore" those who are sanctified in Him are called to go forth to Him "without the camp." There can be no association of those sanctified by His blood with the city that was guilty of His death. The believers had hitherto been associated with the saved remnant of the nation in Jerusalem by baptism with water, as recorded all through "the Acts." But the principle upon which the Church of God is established among the Gentiles is that of "union with Christ as His body," and therefore in separation from Jerusalem, the city which had cast Him out. Hence, Paul writes: "Christ sent me not to baptize, but to preach the Gospel" (1 Cor. 1:17).

The preaching of the Gospel is, therefore, what is specially committed to the Gentiles, for every fresh revelation of truth has its practical result. When justification in Christ was proclaimed to Gentiles and Jews alike in Acts 13:39, it was quickly decreed that the Gentile believers were not to be circumcised, for that would have brought them under the law from which they were justified through faith in Christ. So when the saints are declared to be sanctified in Christ, the washing of the flesh in water, the ceremonial rite of sanctification, is ended: for Christ, by the offering of His body once, "hath perfected forever those that are sanctified" as regards ordinances upon the flesh. "having abolished them in His death" (Eph. 2:15).

Now that the Church of God is established among the Gentiles as the Body of Christ (Mystical), it bears the same title as the Lord Jesus applied to His body (personal) when on earth. "He spake of the temple of His body" (John 2:21). Paul says to the saints, "Know ye not that ye are the temple of God?" (1 Cor. 3:16) and "Ye are the body of Christ" (chap. 12:27).

The change in the character of the Church from that of "the camp" to that of "the temple" and of "the body" outside the camp, of which this epistle marks the epoch, is plainly taught in chap. 10. The circumstances of Israel in the wilderness are spoken of, and twice it is said (vs. 6 and 11) these things are our types. Then, in v. 17, it is said: "We being many are one loaf, and one body; for we are all partakers of that one loaf."

The Headship of Christ is the subject of chap. 11; and the order for the Church which is His body, when the members come together into one place, is given by revelation from the Lord. The Lord's table is separated from the Passover supper with which it had always hitherto been associated. "When ye come together therefore into one place this is not to eat a Lordly supper."

The Passover supper was a memorial of Israel's deliverance by power, of the triumph over their enemies. The Lord's table is set among the Gentiles consequent upon Israel's rejection and dispersion, the memorial of His death who came to deliver them. It is to be continued so until He come; it is the token that Christ is no more in the world but gone again to the Father who sent Him (John 17:11). The saints who are partakers of it are "sanctified in Christ," for they are identified with the sacrifice of Him "who through the eternal Spirit offered Himself without spot to God"; they are the "members of His body," who suffered without the gate that He might sanctify them with His own blood.

To eat of this bread and to drink of this cup as in any way associated with *the city that cast Him out*, is to eat and drink unworthily and to be guilty of His death. For those who are the partakers of the altar and are accepted in the beloved one and in His one offering, dishonour Him if associated with the city in separation from which He offered Himself. Union with Christ, in separation from Jerusalem, is a first principle of the Church of God among the Gentiles, sanctified in Christ, calling upon the name of the Lord Jesus.

Chapter 12 shows the constitution of the Church of God and how those who were Gentiles have come to call on the name of Christ Jesus our Lord. "No man can say that Jesus is Lord (*i.e.* take Him as Master and Head), but by the Holy Ghost."

While the Church had its centre in Jerusalem, the Gentile believers were associated with the saved remnant of Israel by baptism in confession of Jesus as the Lord: but Paul was not sent to establish the Church of God among the Gentiles as such an assembly. They were not to be known after the flesh, or by ordinances connected with the flesh, since Christ is no more known after the flesh (2 Cor. 5:16), but by the *manifestation of the Spirit* in each one of those who are members of the body of Christ. "For with one Spirit are we all baptized into one body, whether Jews or Gentiles, whether bond or free; and have all been made to drink into one spirit." Jesus, the ascended Lord and Christ, is the one Baptizer, who has baptized into one body all those who by the Holy Spirit confess Him to be the one Lord. This is the one faith of the Church of God (Eph. 4:5), the confession of every member of the body of Christ.

Chapter 13 teaches that love is to be the ruling principle among the saints; this is according to the Lord's commandment in John 13:34; it teaches also that the speaking with tongues, which together with baptism accompanied the confession of Christ during the preaching of the kingdom of God, shall cease. The ordinance connected with the flesh and the outward signs of power end when the Church is established among the Gentiles as the body of Christ.

Doubtless those who had received the miraculous gifts, speaking with tongues, etc. retained them, so chap. 14 gives instruction for their proper use in the Church, while those who possess them remain; but there is no Scripture to indicate that they were *given* after the Church was established as the body of Christ among the Gentiles.

Paul did not lay hands on Epaphroditus to heal him, when sick nigh unto death (Phil. 2:27), nor upon Timothy for the weakness of his stomach (1 Tim. 5:23).

In 1 Cor.15 Paul recounts to them the Gospel which he had preached to them. "I delivered unto you first of all that which I also received how that Christ died for our sins according to the Scriptures; and that He was buried, and that He rose again the third day according to the Scripture."

He shows that the resurrection of the Lord Jesus is the great fact upon which the whole truth of the Gospel rests. He then adds (v. 51): "Behold, I show you a mystery; we shall not all sleep, but we shall all be changed, in a moment, in the twinkling of an eye at the last trump: for the trumpet shall sound, and the dead shall be raised incorruptible, and we shall be changed."

In chap. 16:8, Paul writes: "But I will tarry at Ephesus until Pentecost." This is proof that the epistle was written after Paul had ceased preaching in the synagogues (Acts 19:20), and before he departed from Ephesus in Acts 20:1. It shows beyond dispute that the preaching of the kingdom as a public testimony to the Jews was ended (Acts 19:20) before "the Mystery" was revealed to the Gentiles, establishing the Church as the body of Christ.[2]

---

[2] Editor's note: Bullinger was later to change his position on this point, seeing Paul continuing his ministry of preaching the kingdom to the Jews right up to the end of Acts (see Acts 28:17-23) and "the Mystery" establishing the Church as the body of Christ coming at Acts 28:28. These views can be seen in his last book *The Foundations of Dispensational Truth*: details of this publication can be seen at the end of this book.

# PERFECTION.

# PERFECTION.

In a recent number wrote on the words. "Be Perfect." We propose now to take the noun "Perfection." When we are dealing with human words, and the words relate to truths which are infinite and Divine, the task is no light one. And when we add that there are ten Hebrew words in the Old Testament, and four in the New Testament used for the adjective *"perfect"*: four Hebrew Old Testament words, and four Greek New Testament words used for the words, *"be perfect"*: while five Hebrew Old Testament words and five New Testament words used for the noun *"perfection."* it will be seen that the subject is by no means small.

One thing invests this and all similar subjects with great solemnity, and that is, we are dealing with "the words which the Holy Ghost teacheth." and are thus standing on holy ground.

Though we shall confine ourselves to the New Testament it is interesting to notice some of the Old Testament words in passing.

Jer. 23:20: "In the latter days ye shall consider it *perfectly"* Here the Hebrew word is *'been' to make to understand,* and means ye shall consider it intelligently i.e., so as to understand it.

Ps. 138:8: "The Lord will *perfect* that which concerneth me." Here the word is the Hebrew word *'gamar' to finish* or *complete* and teaches the same truth as Phil. 1:6 (and margin), showing that whatever the Lord doeth it is forever.

Prov. 4:18: "The path of the just is as the shining light that shineth more and more unto the *perfect* day." Here the word means *prepared* and also *established*.

When we come to the New Testament we find variety also, though not so great. There are two classes of words the meanings which are governed by their respective roots; and one or two separate words.

The two Greek roots are '*telos*' and '*artios*'. The former always has the idea of end and the latter of fitness.

*Telos* is the word put by the Greeks at the end of a book; just as the Latins put *Finis*, and we put *The End.*

Therefore, the Greek noun '*teleios*' means *that which has reached its end* (as a book): that which has reached its limit.

The Greek verb '*teleivõ*' means *to bring or come to the end; i.e.,* complete.

What the *end* may be the word by itself never tells us. It always depends on the context, and we must always look out for it in the subject which is being treated. For example, in -

# HEBREWS 9:9

The Holy Spirit is speaking of sacrifices, baptisms, rites, and ordinances, "that could not make him that did the service perfect as pertaining to the conscience."

The contrast here is plainly between the sacrifices of the law and Christ (v. 11). "The law ... can never, with those sacrifices which they offered year by year continually, make the comers thereunto perfect" (Heb. 10:1). Why not? Because they were never ended. No one could ever write *telos* or *finis* against them. Then how could the comers thereunto ever write *telos* or *finis* as regards the conscience?

The meaning of the word "perfect" here is clear, and its essence as meaning *end* is evident. A reference to John 19:28 makes it still plainer, for there we have the verb, and a reference to the one sacrifice which in Heb. 9 is set in contrast to those offered under the law. "Jesus, knowing that all things were now accomplished, (see in the Greek '*tetelesthai*') that the Scripture might be fulfilled, (Greek '*teleiōthee*') saith, thirst."

Here were two things *finished* and brought to an end; the work which the Lord Jesus came to do, and the prophecy of Psa. 69:21. Therefore *finis* can be written against all schemes for giving "the guilty conscience peace." All are vain and worse than useless, for they are a denial of the blessed fact that God has written *telos* or *finis* on Christ's meritorious death; and all ignore the Saviour's dying words – "It is finished."[3]

The sinner who rests on a finished work must have a finished conscience. Nothing can be put to it or taken from it. The sacrifice is perfect in that sense; and therefore, in the same sense, the conscience of the saved sinner must be perfect also: *i.e.,* in proportion as he realises that nothing is left to be done by Christ, or himself, or anyone, or anything else, and in proportion as he realizes that *finis* is written on that precious death of our Saviour Christ.

If the sinner does not realize this, then he seeks, by observing "Rules for daily living," or by the observance of rites and ceremonies, to obtain a perfect conscience. We need not add that he seeks in vain, for in ourselves "there dwelleth no good thing."

## PHILIPPIANS 3:12

"Not as though I did already attain (*those gains which have in Christ,* for which I count my former gains but loss) either have already reached the end (of my gains)."

Here the context shows that the whole subject of the chapter is concerning what Paul had given up as a Jew, and now counted loss in comparison with the "gains" which he had in Christ.

---

[3] This is from the same root, *finis:* hence, finis-hed.

All these gains were in Christ, and all the excellency of knowledge was bound up in Him. That knowledge consisted of knowing Him as his righteousness ("found in Him" v. 9). Knowing Him in His person, experiencing the power of His resurrection, sharing the fellowship of His sufferings, made conformable unto His death. All these were past and present blessings, but there were two future: resurrection and rapture (vs. 11 and 20, 21; compare 1 Thess. 4:16, 17).

Paul had all in Christ. He had written *finis* as to all earthly gains and all earthly knowledge. He had written *telos* as to all other objects for the heart, for Christ was the end of both one and the other. Christ's *work* is an end of all objects as to the conscience, and Christ's person is the end of all objects for the heart. The blood of Christ gives us a perfect conscience, and the Person of Christ furnishes us with a perfect object.

## MATTHEW 5:48

"Be ye therefore perfect, even as your Father which is in heaven is perfect."

Here the word has the same interpretation; and the word "therefore" shows us to what it points. The perfection here is not absolute but relative and is limited by the context to our dealings with others. Our Father is dealing in grace and causing His sun to shine, and His showers to fall on the evil and on the good, on the just and on the unjust. Let us do likewise. Let us act on this same principle of grace, and we can then write "*finis*" and "*telos*," on all other principles which may be taken as guides for our walk. The perfection referred to here does not go beyond this principle.

## REVELATION 3:2

"I have not found thy works perfect before God." Here we have a different word altogether. It is in the Greek *'pleeroõ'*; and is the ordinary word for *fulfil* in connection with prophecy; it is so rendered fifty times. So here it means fulfilled, *i.e., performed* before God, with a single eye to His glory. If in Matt. 5:48 we had a word as to the principle which is to govern our *walk*, here we have a principle which is to govern our *service*. Both are perfect if God's grace produces the one, and God's glory is the aim of the other.

## 2 TIMOTHY 3:17

"That the man of God may be perfect." Here we have another Greek word *'artios'* which, although it is used only here, yet gives its character to another class of words when used in combination and used as verbs.

It is from the old Aryan root *'ar', to fit,* and the obsolete Greek verb *'arõ', to fit.*

*'artios'* means that which exactly fits, fitting like a joint.

Of *time* the Greeks used it of the very point or "nick" of time. Of *numbers* it meant *even* as opposed to odd, etc.

Used in connection with the Word of God, it teaches us that the man of God who is versed in the Scriptures, subject to them, profited by them, and instructed in them is perfect, *i.e.* he has a perfect rule of life. He can write *finis* as to all other rules. He can write *telos* as to all other guides. There is an *end of* all of them. He is ready for every emergency, equipped for every exigency, prepared for every difficulty, provided for every contingency.

He needs no "rules for daily living." To adopt any of them is to practically deny that the Word of God is sufficient.

Having this we are prepared for eternity as well as time: for it tells us what we have to wait for, and that is …

# PERFECTION IN GLORY.

# PERFECTION IN GLORY.

We grasp at the blessed promise of 1 Cor. 13:9, 10. Now we know in part, "but when that which is perfect is come, then that which in part shall be done away." What a precious revelation. That which is perfect is coming. Glorious news! For it means that the Perfect One Himself is coming! And till He comes there is no hope for the Jew, no hope for the Gentile, no hope for the Church of God. He only has the right, and He only has the might to bring in the perfect age. Hence, we wait and we groan, waiting for the dawn of the perfect day.

---

## HOSEA 3:4,5

In this passage we have a wonderful prophecy concerning Israel, the importance of which is contained in the word "abide."

We will first set out these two verses according to their structure. They begin with "for" because they are the explanation of the symbolical action of verses 1-3.

A₁  For many days[4]

    B₁    a  the children of Israel[4]

          b  shall abide[4]

             c  without a king, without a prince,
                without a sacrifice, and without a
                statue, and without ephod and
                teraphim.

A₂  Afterwards

    B₂    *a*  the children of Israel[4]

          *b*  shall return and seek[4]

             *c*  Jehovah their God, and David
                  their king, and shall rejoice in
                  Jehovah and his goodness.

A₃  in the latter days.

Here we notice (in A₁, A₂, A₃) three marks of time, followed by two alternate extended parallelisms. In these we have two great facts set forth as to the *present* and *future* condition of Israel. When the words were spoken by Jehovah, what is now present was then future.

In "*c*" and "*c*" of each pair we have the description of what should characterise the respective conditions during the "many days" (A₁); "afterwards," (A₂); and "at the end of the days" (A₃). In B₁ we have their *abiding*, and in B₂ their *return*.

---

[4] We have reversed the order of the Hebrew of these words so as to accord with our English idiom.

Each part of this description (c and *c*) consists of three pairs, which set forth the conditions.

c   "King and prince." Civil government should cease.
"Sacrifice and statue." Religious worship, true and false, should cease, for the Hebrew word '*matzevah*', is connected with idolatrous worship (Ex. 23:24), and was therefore forbidden (Lev. 26:1, Deut. 16:22; see 1 Kings 14:23, etc.).

"Ephod and Teraphim": *i.e.*, all idolatrous emblems should cease; see Judges 17:5; 18:14.

And after these "many days" it is not a negative description of *things* that is given, but a positive description of acts. They shall *return, seek,* and *rejoice.* Here again we have three pairs, marked by three possessive pronouns:

c   "Jehovah their God"
"David their king," and
"Jehovah and His goodness."

This mention of David refers especially to the Ten Tribes, who will seek; their true king in David's line, and be no more a separate kingdom, but joined, and made "one stick" with Judah.

There are two words now to be considered:

1.     The word rendered "abide." It is not in the Hebrew *'bo'*, *to come in* or *enter*; not *'gur'*, *to sojourn*; not *'chul'*, *to stay* or *rest*; *not 'chanah'* *to rest* after travelling; not *'lm'*, *to lodge*; not any other of many synonyms, but it is *'yashav'*, *to sit*, or *settle down, abide*. It is rendered *dwell* 444 times; *abide*, 69 times; *sit down,* 20 times; *remain,* 23 times, etc. Its first occurrence is Gen. 4:16. Compare Gen. 47:11, Ps. 102:12 (endure); 29:10 (sitteth), for its usage.

The great point of the prophecy is this; that though Israel has lost everything nationally, king, prince, temple, sacrifice, and all religious emblems, and has been scattered among all nations, and dissolved into individuals, yet the wonderful fact is that Israel still *abides*! No example of the kind exists in history. Nothing similar has ever happened before with regard to any people. No human foresight could have predicted it. Israel is "scattered," and yet "dwells alone" (Num. 23:9). Everything, civil and religious, has been swept away, but Israel *abides* without even idolatrous worship to hold the people together (as devised by Jeroboam, who saw the necessity of some such bond of union).

Yes, "Israel," and not merely Judah, and therefore not "British" or any other "Israel"! For *we* have kings and princes, and national religion, and religious symbols in abundance, and hence, necessarily are entirely shut out. Anglo-Israelites boast that Queen Victoria is in David's line. They have no King to "seek" therefore. And their whole claim to be Israel is crushed by this verse.

2.    The other word is "shall fear," in Hebrew *'pachad'*. But this is a *homonym*: *i.e.,* a word spelt like another word with a different meaning (like our English word "let"; one means to *hinder*, and another spelt just the same means *to allow*; or the word "repair" which means *to renew*, and another *to resort*).[5]

So here, one-word *pachad* means *to fear*, as in Deut. 28:66 and Job 23:15, and the other *pachad* means *to rejoice* or *praise,* as in Isa. 60:5, Jer. 23:9 and Hos. 3:5. This agrees with the scope of the passage: for Israel will *rejoice* in Jehovah's "goodness," but hardly "fear" it!

Thus the study of these two words helps us to a clearer understanding of this remarkable prophecy; and helps also to assure us that, as the abiding many days in this condition has been fulfilled to the very letter, so will the *returning* be literal –"afterwards," "at the end of the days." Already we see many signs, not indeed of the returning to Jehovah, but of the returning to the Land, and this will surely lead to the other, for it is written, "I will take you from among the heathen, and gather you out of all countries, and will bring you into your own LAND, - THEN will I sprinkle clean water upon you." etc. (Ezek. 36:24, 25.)

---

[5] See E W Bullinger's *Figures of Speech*, Appendix D.

# ABOUT THE AUTHOR

Ethelbert W. Bullinger D.D. (1837-1913) was a direct descendant of Heinrich Bullinger, the great Swiss reformer who carried on Zwingli's work after the latter had been killed in war.

E. W. Bullinger was brought up a Methodist but sang in the choir of Canterbury Cathedral in Kent. He trained for and became an Anglican (Episcopalian) minister before becoming Secretary of the Trinitarian Bible Society. He was a man of intense spirituality and made a number of outstanding contributions to biblical scholarship and broad-based evangelical Christianity.

Some of the works of E W Bullinger published by The Open Bible Trust include:

The Transfiguration
The Knowledge of God
God's Purpose in Israel
The Lord's Day (Revelation 1:10)
The Rich Man and Lazarus
The Importance of Accuracy
Christ's Prophetic Teaching
The Prayers of Ephesians
The Resurrection of the Body
The Spirits in Prison: 1 Peter 3:17-4:6
The Christians' Greatest Need
Introducing the Church Epistles
The Second Advent in Relation to the Jew
The Name of Jehovah in the Book of Esther
The Two Natures in the Child of God
The Names and Order of the Books of the Old
Testament
The Foundations of Dispensational Truth
The Road to Holiness
Sanctification and Perfection
The Man of God
The Vail, The Leaven, The Church and Prayer

For details of the above,
and for a full list of his works
published by The Open Bible Trust, please visit

**www.obt.org.uk**

They are available as KDP paperbacks from Amazon,
and also as eBooks from Amazon and Kindle

# ALSO BY E W BULLINGER

## THE FOUNDATIONS OF DISPENSATIONAL TRUTH

This is Bullinger's last book and is his definitive work on the subject of dispensationalism. It covers the ministries of ...

- the prophets,
- the Son of God,
- those that heard Christ, and
- the ministry of Paul, the Apostle to the Gentiles.

He comments on the Gospels and the Pauline epistles and has a lengthy section on the Acts of the Apostles, followed by one explaining why miraculous signs of the Acts period ceased.

A hard-back edition is available from **www.obt.org.uk** and from

The Open Bible Trust,
Fordland Mount, Upper Basildon,
Reading, RG8 8LU, UK.

A newly typeset book, well presented in an easy to read format, is available as a KDP paperback Amazon, which is also available as an eBook from Amazon and Kindle.

\*\*\*\*\*\*\*\*\*

Readers may also care to obtain a copy of *The Development of Dispensationalism* by Michael Penny, which make references to E W Bullinger and others.

Again, this is available as a KDP paperback Amazon, and an eBook from Amazon and Kindle.

# THE TWO NATURES IN THE CHILD OF GOD

## By E W Bullinger

The Bible sees the Christian as having an 'old nature', inherited through generation from Adam, and a 'new nature', bestowed through regeneration by God.

The names and characteristics of each are many and various, including "the natural man" and "the old man" over against "the divine nature" and "the new man".

The conflict between the two natures is discussed with details of our responsibilities regarding each, and the ultimate end of the old and new natures.

Finally, practical suggestions are made for dealing with the old nature.

This book is published by The Open Bible Trust.

It is available as an eBook from Apple and Amazon and as a KDP paperback from Amazon.

# ABOUT THIS BOOK

## Sanctification and Perfection

This is a book which will help many 21st Century Christians have a better understanding and appreciation of these two subjects.

What is 'sanctification'? And what does the Bible mean by 'perfection' and being 'perfect'?

Is sanctification a process we go through, or it is something which is given us by God through Christ?

And what about perfection? Is that God-given or do we have to strive towards it|? And is it possible to reach perfection, this side of glory?

This are some of the questions Bullinger deals with and answers in his usual through, Bible-based style.

Publications of The Open Bible Trust must be in accordance with its evangelical, fundamental and dispensational basis. However, beyond this minimum, writers are free to express whatever beliefs they may have as their own understanding, provided that the aim in so doing is to further the object of The Open Bible Trust. A copy of the doctrinal basis is available on **www.obt.org.uk** or from:

**THE OPEN BIBLE TRUST**
**Fordland Mount, Upper Basildon,**
**Reading, RG8 8LU, UK**

Made in the USA
Coppell, TX
10 June 2020